A LOCAL HISTORY OF CAMDEN

COURT HOUSE , CAMDEN

From the 1858 edition.

A LOCAL HISTORY OF CAMDEN,

COMMENCING WITH

ITS EARLY SETTLEMENT,

Incorporation, and Public and Private Improvements,

BROUGHT UP TO THE PRESENT DAY.

BY L. F. FISLER, M. D.

"Who would be without a history of his country?"
—*Franklin.*

Camden, N. J.
FRANCIS A. CASSEDY, PUBLISHER.
1858.

Republished by
The South Jersey Culture & History Center
2024.

This edition published 2024 by South Jersey Culture & History Center

South Jersey Culture & History Center
Stockton University
101 Vera King Farris Drive
Galloway, NJ 08205

Title: A Local History of Camden: Commencing with Its Early Settlement, Incorporation, and Public and Private Improvements, Brought Up To the Present Day

Author: Lorenzo F. Fisler

Additional material Copyright © 2024
ISBN: 978-1-947889-23-1

J. H. Jones & Co., PRINTERS,
No. 34 Carter's Alley, Philada.

A LOCAL HISTORY OF CAMDEN

NEW PREFACE.

I first became aware of Dr. Lorenzo F. Fisler's pamphlet publication, *A Local History of Camden Commencing with Its Early Settlement, Incorporation, and Public and Private Improvements Brought Up to the Present Day*, when I began researching Camden City history some fifty years ago. At the time, I took the pamphlet and its text at face value, but as the reader will find below, I have a somewhat different viewpoint of the work today. While the text has its content shortcomings, it is a rare pamphlet for any New Jerseyana collector to possess and many years had elapsed before I added one to my own library. Given its scarcity, the work is worthy of this reprinting for new generations to read and to learn about the City of Camden from its inception through to the 1850s. The city, as a budding urban center, like many other cities across the country, nucleated around its transportation modalities. As originally presented, Fisler's historical account, *A Local History of Camden…*, first appeared in serial form in the newspaper the *West Jerseyman* during 1856. He then proceeded to publish it as a pamphlet. It is the first stand-alone history to describe Camden City and its rise from a simple colonial ferry hub to a growing urban center in the 1850s.

Some historians often lay a foundation for subsequent historians. Fisler was indebted to the initial work of Isaac Mickle, *Reminiscences of Old Gloucester County*, first published in 1845. A young erudite attorney, Mickle held an abiding interest in local history from an early age, as witnessed in his set of diaries: either the originals at the Camden County Historical Society or the published two-volume set that Philip English Mackey edited and the University of Pennsylvania released. Mickle's early death at age 33 robbed the world of a man whose lengthened shadow would have extended far forward. A review of George R. Prowell's 1886 *History of Camden County, New Jersey* demonstrates that both Mickle and Fisler informed Prowell of the city's history as he prepared to write a traditional late-nineteenth-century county history of the type that proliferated across the nation during the time period.

Fisler commences his narrative with its stated purpose:

> When engaged in the prosecution of my profession, I have frequently employed myself in gathering up a few facts connected with the early history of our city. If my labors shall induce some abler one to pursue these inquiries still further, all will have been accomplished which was designed.

Is this the only reason Fisler proceeded to produce his pamphlet history? Despite his statement of purpose, Dr. Fisler clearly repurposed his series of newspaper articles into a pamphlet for wider circulation to promote the city's growth, i.e., as publicity for a Camden that had become temporarily moribund and stunted following the ferryboat NEW JERSEY burning on a cold and icy March 15, 1856, while crossing to Camden. The devastating conflagration resulted in many deaths and untold injuries, and lasting disabilities from those subjected to lengthy immersion in the frigid river water. Prior to the fire, Camden had become a growing suburb of Philadelphia, with workers taking the twice-daily crossing in stride to travel between home and their employment. Following the ferryboat's burning, however, those people commuting between Camden and Philadelphia suddenly became awakened to the potential dangers of the river crossing, and fear drove them to return to residing in Philadelphia. According to George R. Prowell, writing in his 1886 work, *The History of Camden County, New Jersey*, ". . . lots were sold on easy terms and the sales were rapid until the burning of the ferry-boat "New Jersey," in 1856 . . . checked the inflow of home-seekers from the western shore of the Delaware."

With the extensive coverage that Fisler provides of ferry operations throughout his historical text, there is no mention of the disastrous 1856 fire, which occurred a mere two years prior to the pamphlet's publication. It is entirely plausible that Fisler intentionally paid the ferry operations undue attention as a means of demonstrating the long and relatively safe history the various ferries had provided crossing the Delaware between Camden and Philadelphia. To hold enough space for describing the ferries and their history—fully one-third of the total page count—Fisler limits his retelling of city history and commends his readers to review the retrospective that Isaac Mickle offers on Camden history within his *Reminiscences of Old Gloucester* in substitution. Within the text, Fisler offers an encapsuled account of Camden's many protestant churches. Yet, he curiously fails to mention the city's largest Black church—Macedonia African Methodist Episcopal Church—but then appends a brief description of the edifice to the very end of his narrative as a separate "Appendix." The odd placement of the Macedonia reference at the very end of the work, and that the description is devoid of any reference to the church being African American, is indicative of a major shortcoming in the pamphlet's contents: there is not a single reference to the African Americans residing in and around the city.

A decade later, Alexander Barrington Irvine, writing under the pseudonym Carnesworthe, drafted a similar historical publicity piece titled *Atlantic City: Its Early and Modern History*. Written in a more jocular style, it appears the Camden & Atlantic Railroad commissioned Irvine to prepare his text in support of passenger service and city growth. Perhaps Irvine loosely patterned his work after what Fisler had prepared.

Dr. Lorenzo Felix Fisler was born near Fislerville (present-day Clayton), in Franklin Township, Gloucester County, New Jersey, to Dr. Benjamin Fisler Sr. and

Catherine Murphy Fisler in April 1797. After receiving his primary and secondary education, he determined to follow in his father's footsteps and attended the University of Pennsylvania for his medical training, graduating in 1818. In 1825, he received his license to practice from the Salem County Board of Censors and the New Jersey Medical Society appointed him to that very same board in 1829. At the age of 32, he wedded Anna Maria Risley in May 1830 while residing in Maurice River Township, Cumberland County. The marriage produced five children. Lorenzo and his family moved to Camden in 1835. In 1846, Dr. Fisler was one of the signatories in founding the Camden County Medical Society, but his name was erased from the commission received from the state medical society and Dr. James S. Risley's name substituted. With the society duly constituted, it proceeded to establish a Board of Censors, which published a list of licensed physicians, omitting Lorenzo Fisler from the list due to him having misplaced his license issued in 1825 and testimony against Fisler from Dr. Hannah of Salem County. At this time, he had practiced medicine for 28 years, eleven of which he spent in Camden. As a result of these two slights, Dr. Fisler refused to join the county medical society, although he was a well-known member of the state society. Despite apologies and attempts to make amends, Fisler remained resolute and never joined the Camden County Medical Society.

In public service, Lorenzo Fisler served as Camden's mayor for seven terms and also held a seat in city council. He engaged in promoting various charities that appealed to his sense of fairness and public duty. Dr. Fisler lived a long and productive life before his demise on March 29, 1871, at the age of 74. He lies in repose within the family plot at the Port Elizabeth United Methodist Churchyard, Cumberland County, New Jersey. At an adjourned meeting of the Camden City Council held on April 6 following Lorenzo's death, the following occurred:

> Mr. Goldthorp offered a resolution of respect to the memory of Lorenzo F. Fisler, M.D., a resident of Camden for many years, and its executive officer seven times.
>
> Mr. Bourquin made a few appropriate remarks and gave the Doctor the praise of writing the only authentic history of Camden. It was unanimously passed. (*The Camden Democrat*, April 8, 1871, page [3])

Notwithstanding the shortcomings in Fisler's text, and now possessing the probable purpose of its original publication, this reprint is long overdue. May present and future historians of Camden and the Delaware Valley place this pioneering work near the top of their literature search.

PAUL W. SCHOPP.
November 5, 2023.

THE PUBLISHER'S INTRODUCTION.

In presenting to the citizens of Camden the history of our growing city, the Publisher, with great pleasure, takes this opportunity of respectfully returning his sincere thanks to those persons who have sustained and encouraged him in the work. He trusts it will not only prove acceptable to those liberal-minded citizens and others whose names have already been enrolled upon its subscription list, but to those, also, who design, but have not, as yet, had the opportunity of adding their names to those already received.

The Publisher would here express his grateful acknowledgements to the gentleman who has, in so generous a manner, presented to us this history of our city, it being the fruit of long and patient research, and often pursued amid official cares and professional duties. There seems to be a peculiar fitness in this contribution which the author now makes to the local literature of Camden, he having presided over her interests for many years as her chief magistrate.

FRANCIS A. CASSEDY.
July 1, 1858.

TO THE HONORABLE PRESIDENT AND MEMBERS

OF THE

CITY COUNCIL OF CAMDEN

Gentlemen:—The present History of our city has been thoroughly revised, rewritten, and much enlarged by the addition of valuable matter. It is now submitted to the public as a record of many important events connected with our early history. I can truly say that my only design in its publication is, to secure to the future some important facts which must soon pass away and be forgotten. To you who have so kindly aided me in this little work, I here beg leave to acknowledge my indebtedness, and to you is it most respectfully inscribed by

THE AUTHOR.
Camden, July 1, 1858.

A LOCAL HISTORY OF CAMDEN.

When engaged in the prosecution of my profession, I have frequently employed myself in gathering up a few facts connected with the early history of our city. If my labors shall induce some abler one to pursue these inquiries still further, all will have been accomplished which was designed.

It is proposed to present to my readers a brief outline of Camden, commencing with her early settlement, up to her incorporation and to the present day. My remarks on this first head will be but general; referring you for further information on this subject to an interesting work entitled *Reminiscences of Old Gloucester*, written by the late ISAAC MICKLE, Esq. It contains a great amount of valuable matter in relation to my native county. I shall more particularly confine myself to within that period of time in which I have had the honor to hold a citizenship in Camden. It may be that there are those who are somewhat familiar with these matters; those I may not be able to interest, but there is a large number of my readers whose attention I hope to secure, and if I shall succeed in imparting a small degree of the pleasure that has been realized in gathering up a few fragments of an age that must soon be forgotten, then my effort will not have been unrewarded.

Camden, anterior to the charter of incorporation, which constituted her a city, was a small and unimportant village, situated in the county of Gloucester, and the township of Newton. It contained at that time but a few houses and a population proportionably small. Without business, and without the least spark or spirit or enterprise, for years she was content to remain a mere thoroughfare, through which hundreds daily passed to and from the great business mart on the opposite shore of the Delaware. What little importance she then possessed was solely dependent on her proximity to Philadelphia. Camden, in the original town plot, was of very limited dimensions. On the north it was bounded by the south side of Cooper street, extending down to a line running about midway between Market and Plum streets, and from the Delaware river to Sixth street. These were the outlines, as laid down in the original survey of the town. All outside of these bounds, with the exception of a few houses, were either sterile fields or thick forests of trees. What few dwellings there were, were mostly along the margin of the river, and occupied by fishermen and ferrymen.

About the year 1814, Edward Sharp, Esq., a wealthy gentleman, who then resided at the northeast center of Second and Cooper streets, purchased of Joshua Cooper all the land lying between Federal street, down to Line street, South Camden. It was the intention of Mr. Sharp to construct a bridge from Camden over to Windmill Island, for which purpose a street of one hundred and twenty feet in width was laid out, called

18

"Bridge avenue," at the foot of which the bridge was to start. A charter for it was granted on the 26th of January, 1819, by our Legislature, but the projectors were unable to dispose of the stock, and therefore the enterprise resulted in a total failure.

CHURCHES.

We have little or no account of any schools or churches until about the year 1809, at which time a lot of ground was purchased of Joshua Cooper, on the northwest corner of Fourth and Federal streets, on which to erect a Methodist Episcopal Church. Prior to this time, there were occasional meetings of this society, held in private houses.

On the 25th of November, 1810, their new house was dedicated. Its dimensions were just thirty feet square. On this occasion the Rev. Thomas Dunn preached an appropriate discourse, taking for his text these words from the book of Ezra:—"*Who hath commanded you to build this house and to make these walls?*"

The pulpit of that old building had often been filled by men, inferior in zeal and piety to none of the present day, and though they have all since gone to "reap their reward," yet their memories are still loved and cherished, and the names of Thomas Dunn, Joseph Rusling, Joseph Lybrand and many others, will always be ranked among the first and faithful heralds of early *Methodism* in Camden.

After the lapse of years, this house was found insufficient to meet the wants of this young and increasing denomination. The old building was disposed of, and in 1834 the foundation stone of the present church in Third street was laid. Its dimensions are 52 by 72 feet, with spacious galleries. Its present pastor is the Rev. E. H. Stokes.

The next church which was instituted in Camden was the First Baptist Church, situated in Fourth street, between Market and Plum streets.

In the early part of the year 1818, the following named persons withdrew from the First Baptist Church in Philadelphia and established the above named society:—Sylvanus Sheppard, Phoebe Sheppard, Richard Johnson, Ann Johnson, Isaac Smith, Hannah Ludlam and Eleanor Sheppard. On the 5th of February, 1818, they were regularly constituted, the Revs. Henry Holcombe, D. D., John Sisty and Daniel James officiating. Their first meetings were held in a private dwelling in Plum street, near Fourth.

The Rev. Daniel James assumed the pastoral charge, and at once commenced the erection of a house of worship, which was completed and dedicated towards the close of the year 1818. Its dimensions were 40 by 50 feet. Including the present pastor, the Rev. Stephen H. Murick, the church has had the following named pastors:—Rev. Daniel James, Rev. Thomas J. Kitts, Rev. Charles J. Hopkins, Rev. William S. Hall, Rev. Amassa Smith, Rev. N. B. Tyndale, Rev. Wm. Smith, Rev. Thomas R. Taylor and Rev. John Duncan.

The shortest pastorate was that of the Rev. Daniel James, and the longest that of the Rev. Thomas R.

Taylor; the former continuing but seven months, and the latter eleven years. In February, 1839, a resolution was adopted to demolish this old building, and to rear one of larger proportions. In January, 1841, the present house was dedicated by the Rev. A. D. Gillette. Its dimensions are 45 by 55 feet. So rapidly has this congregation and membership increased within a few years, that it is now contemplated to enlarge the present building by the addition of 25 feet to the rear end of it.

The Episcopal denomination was without a church until the year 1834; though for some time previous religious exercises were held by this society in the old City Court House. In 1834 the corner-stone of St. Paul's, in Market street, was laid, and in 1835 it was dedicated. The Rev. Samuel Starr became the first pastor; he was succeeded by the Rev. Francis P. Lee; afterwards by the Rev. Henry Burroughs; then by the Rev. Joseph M. Lybrand, and now the Rev. Dr. Jos. F. Garrison.

Within a few years, a second Episcopal congregation has been organized, who purchased the *Floating Chapel,* and placed it on Broadway, ornamenting and improving that beautiful part of our city. Its pastor is the Rev. Elvin K. Smith.

About the year 1827, at the time of the unhappy difficulties which arose among the Society of Friends, a branch of them erected a place of worship in Market street, far out in the outskirts of the town. For years its plain and simple structure was concealed within the shade of the thick forests of trees which then surrounded it, but its still and quiet retreat has long since been invaded by the march of improvement.

The First Presbyterian Church of Camden was organized by the Presbytery of West New Jersey, September 27th, 1840, at which time it consisted of twelve members. The Rev. William L. McCalla acted as stated supply for several months. An effort was then made to erect a church edifice, which resulted in a failure, and the Society was temporarily disbanded in December, 1841.

With renewed efforts another organization was effected in June, 1846, under the immediate superin- tendence of the Rev. Giles Manwarring, who became the first pastor, and was installed April 13th, 1847, by the Presbytery of West New Jersey. When the Rev. Mr. Manwarring commenced his labors in this city, he knew of but two Presbyterian families in the whole town. Divine service was first held in a school room, in Third street, between Market and Plum streets. For a considerable time the number of worshipers varied from eight to twenty, including children. In 1846, they commenced worshiping in the City Court House, in Federal street, and so continued until 1847. Here the congregation increased so much that application was made to the Presbytery to be organized into a church. In the meantime, the foundation of a church edifice was laid, and, by the untiring efforts of the first pastor, the work was so far advanced that, in the Spring of 1847, the congregation was enabled to worship in the lecture room of the present edifice, on Fifth street, above Market street, to the erection of which the citizens of Camden and Philadelphia had largely contributed.

After the resignation of Mr. Manwarring, the Rev. Robinson P. Dunn was called to occupy the pulpit. He entered on his labors the last Sabbath in June, 1848, and continued his services with great acceptance until April, 1851, when he received a professorship in "Brown University," Providence, R. I. Mr. Dunn was succeeded by the Rev. Levi H. Christian, who continued his services from July 1, 1851, to December 13, 1853.

The present pastor of this church is the Rev. Daniel Stewart, D. D., who began his labors in March, 1854, but was not formally installed over the church until June 12th, 1856.

This church edifice has been recently greatly enlarged, to the extent of nearly double its former capacity. The lecture room is handsomely fitted up, and under the ministrations of its able and eloquent divine, the congregation has more than doubled its members, and altogether it presents, internally and externally, one of the most attractive churches in our city.

The Second Baptist Church of Camden.—In consequence of the rapid growth of South Camden, a number of Baptists, residing in that part of our city, seeing the necessity of having a place of worship in their own immediate neighborhood, determined to make an effort, which resulted in the building of a house of worship, which is located at the corner of Fourth and Division streets. The edifice is a neat brick building, forty by fifty feet, with a commodious basement beneath. Fifty-four members drew their letters of dismission from the First Baptist Church of North Camden, and the corner-stone was laid in 1848, with appropriate exercises, by the Rev. M. Semple, who became the first pastor. After his resignation, he was succeeded by the Rev. A. E. Clark, in 1850. The congregation worshipped in the basement until the pastorate of the Rev. T. C. Trotter, who was its third pastor. In November, 1852, the church edifice was completed and dedicated, and the Rev. T. Goodwin became the pastor, and so continued for the term of two years. In January, 1855, the Rev. F. T. Cailhopper assumed the charge, and is still the present pastor. Its membership amounts to over two hundred.

The Union Methodist Episcopal Church is situated on the corner of Fifth and Chew streets, South Camden. This society was organized, and the corner-stone of the church laid, in 1848, by the Rev. David W. Bartine. The house was completed and dedicated on the 25th of December, 1848, by the Rev. Charles Pitman, D. D., assisted by the Rev. Wm. P. Corbit. The Rev. Israel S. Corbit was appointed in charge, and was succeeded in 1849 by Rev. W. H. Jefferies. In 1850 this church became a separate charge, by severing its former connection with its old alma mater in Third street. The Rev. David Duffell now became its pastor; who was followed in 1852 by Rev. George Hitchens, in 1854 by Rev. P. Cline, in 1856 by Rev. J. W. Hickman, in 1858 by Rev. H. M. Brown.

Broadway Methodist Episcopal Church is situated on the corner of Berkley street and Broadway. This congregation was organized May 9th, 1854, by Isaac N. Felch, Presiding Elder; it numbered forty members, and Ralph S. Arnett was pastor. The corner-stone of the present church building was laid the 7th of August, 1855, by "*Bishop Janes.*" The lecture room was opened and dedicated for religious worship on the 25th of December, 1855, by "*Bishop Scott*"; Joseph H. Knowles being the pastor. On the 29th of January, 1857, the main audience room was opened, and dedicated by "*Bishop Janes*" and Joseph J. Hanly, the pastor. Its dimensions are forty-nine by fifty-eight feet. On the first floor are the pastor's study, class rooms, lecture room, and infant school room. Caleb R. Fleming is the present pastor. Its membership at the present time is two hundred and fifty-six members. This is one of the most beautiful church edifices in our city.

The Central Presbyterian Church (New School) is situated at the corner of Fourth and Hartman streets, Cooper's Hill. In June, 1851, the corner-stone of this building was laid; Rev. Albert Barnes, Brainard, and others, officiating. In 1852, the Rev. J. W. Mears was ordained and installed its pastor. He was succeeded by the Rev. Mr. Dixon. In the Spring of 1854 the Rev. Mr. Jarvis took charge. This is a beautiful little edifice, constructed entirely of wood, and of the gothic style of architecture. Its height from the floor to the peak of the roof is twenty-eight feet; the dimensions of the whole are: principal building, sixty by thirty feet; portico, seven by eleven feet; semicircular recess for the pulpit, eight feet six inches. The lecture room is eighteen by twenty-five feet, communicating with the main building, and capable, if necessary, of being thrown into one apartment with it. All the materials are of the best quality, the foundations heavy, and the walls and roofing substantial.*

A neat little *German Methodist Church* has recently been organized. It is situated at the corner of Fifth and Line streets. Its dimensions are thirty-four by thirty-six feet, being composed of brick. It numbers about forty members, and the Rev. Mr. Hinkle is the present pastor.

———

PUBLIC BUILDINGS.

The Camden County Court House.—This is among the largest and most substantial edifices to be found in the southern part of our State. This building was commenced in May, 1852, and completed in November, 1853. The dimensions are as follows: sixty feet wide and one hundred and eight feet deep, with a portico on the eastern front, projecting eight feet by thirty-six feet six inches. A basement extends throughout the extent of the building, one portion of which contains twelve cells, and a space under the corridors is apportioned for the reception of the furnaces; the remaining apartments are occupied by the keeper and his family. The first story contains the Surrogate's office, the office of the County Clerk, Orphan's Court room, Sheriff's office, and County Collector's office. The

---

* This building has recently been purchased by the Board of Education, and there is now established in it one of he most valuable and flourishing public schools in our city.

main and private stairways run each way throughout the building. The principal story contains the main court room, Attorney General's room, library, and witnesses' rooms. The petit jury apartments are on the second floor. DANIEL A. HALL, Esq., was the contractor and builder.

No building in our city reflects more credit on the enterprise and spirit of our citizens than that of the *Public School House*, located in the southern portion of our city. It is large, and very substantially built, admirably answering the design for which it was intended. It was erected in the year 1853, and its dimensions are eighty feet square.

The Washington Hall is another public building, situated in the South Ward, at the corner of Fourth and Spruce streets. This is a large three-storied brick building, and has been found very useful for holding public meetings, assemblies, entertainments, &c., &c.

The Odd Fellows' Hall is at the corner of Fourth and Market streets, North Camden. The corner-stone of this building was laid on Thursday, October 5th, 1848, HORN K. KNEASS, Esq., officiating, and was dedicated November 8th, 1849. A great number of Lodges were in attendance, both from Philadelphia and the surrounding country. Its dimensions are thirty-six by sixty feet, three stories in height.

There is an old brick Academy standing at the corner of Market and Sixth street; this was erected at a very early day, in 1803, by subscription of the inhabitants of Camden, and is now employed as a public school house. There are two Market Houses, both of which are situated in Third street, between Market and Federal, and both of which are well patronized.

There are two banking houses in Camden, both of which are beautiful buildings. The "State Bank of Camden" is situated at the corner of Market and Second streets, and the "Farmers' and Mechanics' Bank," (a new institution), at the corner of Market and Front streets.

The "Camden Mutual Fire Insurance Company" have now in progress a commodious building at the corner of Fifth and Federal streets, a part of which is to be appropriated to the transaction of their business, attached to which are several commodious offices.

FERRIES.

At the time at which my remarks commence with Camden, there were five ferries. The one at the foot of Federal street was kept by Joshua Cooper, and then by his son William, and afterwards by Joseph Wilds, and later still by Benjamin Reeves. This old ferry house, now occupied by Parsons and Smith as a hotel, has inserted in its front wall a "tablet," lettered thus:—

"D. M. C."

"1764."

The initials, no doubt, of Daniel Cooper and wife. This is one of the oldest buildings in our city.

At the foot of Market street, North Camden, there were two ferries; the lower one was kept by Peter Farrow, who was succeeded by William Paul, and after him by Benjamin Springer. The ferry on the upper side of the street, where the old stone store house now stands, was in the occupancy of Randal Sparks, and was known by the name of Sparks' ferry.

Cooper street ferry was occupied by James Springer, and after his death by Benjamin Reeves, and Cooper's Point by William Cooper.

There was also, at a very early day, a ferry at Kaighn's Point. It was established in the autumn of 1809, by Joseph Kaighn, who, until that period, had occupied the family mansion connected with his farm, which extended from the river Delaware to the Haddonfield road. Christopher Medara, of Salem county, moved into it, and opened it for the accommodation of the public. The first steamboat at this ferry carried passengers only, and ran to Queen street, Southwark. It is believed that she was named the *Camden.*

In 1815, all the landing and ferrying privileges were leased to a chartered company, called the "Pennsylvania and New Jersey Ferry Company," for the term of 99 years, for a nominal rent, on condition that a good ferry should be maintained by them at that place. The above Company then built the steamboat *Union*; at that time, perhaps, she was the most complete and efficient ferry boat in existence, and would compare favorably with any of the present day. Her commander was the sturdy Captain Burroughs. Her hull was built in Kensington, by Nicholas Vandusen, and her engine, being a very superior one, was constructed at Hoboken, by the late and lamented Robert L. Stevens, Esq., who had then just commenced his active and useful career. She first ran to Washington street, Southwark.

The company, at a great expenditure of money, built substantial piers on both sides of the river, and a large amount of business was done at this ferry; it failed, however, on account, it is said, of a want of a proper economy in its management.

Soon afterwards Washington street was abandoned, and a landing was established at South street. Christopher Medara removed from the hotel in 1816, and was succeeded by George W. Hugg. During his occupancy, Joseph Kaighn sold the property to the widow of Clement Reeves. After a few years, the ferry company forfeited their lease, by failing to run an efficient boat.

Desirous of retaining their lease, after the *Union* had ceased to run, a small steamboat was substituted in her place. This boat was named the *Norristown*. She was built on one of the canals in Pennsylvania. Unfortunately, one night she took fire, while lying in her dock, and was entirely consumed.

The widow Reeves, as before stated, having purchased the ferry property, she, in connection with her son Israel, now became the occupants of the hotel, and in consequence of the interruption in the ferrying operations, she claimed the landing, with all the ferrying privileges appertaining thereto.

This was resisted by the Company, and a law-suit ensued between the parties, which resulted in the widow obtaining the possession of the property. A small steamboat was then constructed, capable of carrying horses, carriages, &c. This boat was named the *New Jersey*.

This hotel, when occupied by George W. Hugg, was very ably kept, and did a very large and prosperous business. "Kaighn's Point" at that day, was a place of great resort for the citizens of Philadelphia during the summer season. It is said that Capt. Watmough, of the "Washington Guards," and Capt. James Page, of the "State Fencibles," often visited this cool and shady retreat, accompanied by Frank Johnson's renowned "Black Band." Then the music consisted of national and patriotic airs and marches, instead of so much of the spiritless stuff of the present day, which has been imported from abroad.

Ebenezer Toole then purchased the property of Mrs. Reeves, and built the steamboat *Kaighn's Point*, commanded by Capt. Benjamin Sutton. The steamer *Southwark* was built after the *New Jersey*, and previous to the *Kaighn's Point*. The next boat was the *Champion*, Capt. Jacob P. Stone, and afterwards Capt. Charles M. Thompson.

The heirs of Ebenezer Toole sold the ferry to the "South Camden Ferry Company," who, in 1853, built the steamer *Stephen Girard*, a boat as convenient and useful as any other that plies between Camden and Philadelphia.

"Cooper's Point Ferry" was always distinguished from all the others by the familiar name of "Upper Billy's." This may have been from the fact that, at one time one of the lower ferries was kept by a person of a similar name, the son of Joshua Cooper. For a number of years "Upper Billy's" was a very popular stopping place for travelers, particularly for Jerseymen.

One reason assigned for this was, and I have often heard it when a boy, that travelers' horses always did their keeper great credit after having been stabled at "Upper Billy's"; their sleek appearance denoting that they had not been stinted in their allotted allowance of corn and oats.

Besides this, Uncle Billy, (as he was universally called,) was a very popular man, and was always ready to meet his visitors with a cordial welcome; and one of his familiar grasps of the hand was not so readily forgotten.

It is said that, during the American revolution, General Abercrombie had his head-quarters at this place, and history informs us that this ground has been trodden by the footsteps of the "Immortal Washington." The foregoing incident is related as having occurred at Cooper's Point, at a time when a part of the British Army were encamped at that place:—While a party of cavalry were engaged in practising their horses in leaping over a hurdle, under the inspection of an officer, the awkwardness of one of these untrained animals caused it to stumble, throwing its rider with some force on the ground. This induced the officer to inquire into the extent of the injury. In reply, he was informed that the man's arm was broken. A party of "Jersey boys" happened to be among the spectators. True to the rebel instinct, which at that time appeared to pervade the whole land, one of the lads, in an undertone of voice, remarked to his comrades that it was a pity "*that it was not his neck.*"

These words met the ear of the officer, but he could not determine which one of the young rascals it was that had given utterance to the treason. They all ran off together, and "Uncle Billy" lived more than a half century afterwards to relate to a friend this amusing little incident of a British officer and of himself.

From the earliest settlement of Camden up to about the year 1810, the crossing of the river was carried on in small boats, which would contain from twelve to fifteen persons. These were called wherries. There were also those of a larger class, named horse boats. These were for the transportation of horses, carriages, cattle, &c. To avoid misapprehension let it be borne in mind that, when horse boats are spoken of, no allusion is intended to those which were propelled by horse-power; these I shall denominate "Team Boats."

Among ferrymen the year was usually divided into two seasons—the Summer and Winter—the former of which commenced about the first of March, and the latter from December to March. During the summer season the rates of ferriage were as follows:—

Each passenger,	$0.12 ½
Wagon and horses,	$1.50
Man and horse,	$0.50
Cattle, per head,	$0.50

and other things in the same proportion.

Throughout the winter these rates were always doubled:—

Single passenger,	$0.25
Wagon and two horses,	$3.00

Man and horse,	$1.00
Cattle, per head,	$1.00

and so on.

No particular time was established for putting on the double rates, or taking them off. This depended somewhat on the weather, and it was generally submitted to the oldest ferry master. It was performed by a certain signal, in the following curious manner:—The horse boats, when not employed, were kept at anchor in the river, opposite the ferry to which they belonged. When anchored out in the Spring, by the direction of the ferry master, that was the signal to all the other ferries to take off the double ferriage; there they lay, when not in service, until the commencement of winter, when they were brought in, and double rates resumed.

In this singular manner the ferrying business was conducted until about the year 1810, at which time a small steamboat made her appearance as a ferry boat. She was commanded by Capt. Ziba Kellum, and was built by Joseph Bispham. She ran from the foot of Cooper street to the lower side of Market street, Philadelphia.

This was the first ferry steamboat that had ever crossed the Delaware river. She was undecked, and carried passengers only. Her name was the *Camden*, and I am glad that she was so called, as she was the early pioneer of steamboating between Camden and Philadelphia.

About the year 1812, a large steamboat commenced running up the river, carrying the New York passengers. This boat was named the *Phoenix*, Capt. Degraw. She ran from Philadelphia to Bordentown, and it took her three hours with the tide, and five against it, to reach her destination. Having no wheel-house, she presented a very singular appearance, as the water, when she was in motion, would often be thrown as high as her smoke pipe. She was sent around here from Hoboken by the elder John Stevens, and Robert L. Stevens was her temporary engineer. She belonged to what was then called the "Swift-Sure Line," and attracted a great deal of curiosity. Her hour of departure was announced by the blowing of a long tin horn, and hundreds of persons would crowd the wharves to see her embark on her perilous voyage. If no accident occurred, her passengers were landed in New York the same day, or else in the course of the night.

Previous to this, passengers were conveyed to Cooper's Point in small boats, and thence in coaches to Amboy, or else in post coaches from Philadelphia to New York, *via* Trenton, Princeton and New Brunswick.

As an evidence of what the facilities for traveling were at that day, and even in after years, I copy the following cards from an old Philadelphia Directory, published in 1818:—

NEW POST CHAISE AND PILOT OFFICE.

Winter Establishment for New York and Baltimore.

The Post Chaise will leave Philadelphia every morning at 5 o'clock, and arrive in New York the same evening, at 6 o'clock.

Fare, $8.00.

SECOND LINE.

The Mail Coach Pilot will leave Philadelphia every afternoon at 2 ½ o'clock, run through, and arrive in New York the next morning. The public are informed that in this line no detention will be met with on the road, as it carries no mail.

Fare, $10.00.

BALTIMORE PILOT

Will leave Philadelphia every morning at 6 o'clock, lodge at Havre De Grace, and arrive in Baltimore next morning by 12 o'clock, (noon).

Fare, $12 00.

It is due to the memory of John Fitch to state, that the first attempt at steamboating on the Delaware river was performed by him as early or about the year 1787. He constructed a boat, and made several trips to Burlington and Trenton, previous to his final abandonment of his long cherished project.

The following highly interesting letter, concerning the unfortunate John Fitch, was published in the *Bucks*

County Intelligencer, at Doylestown, Pa., February 16, 1858, and a copy forwarded to the author:—

Warminster Township,
February 9, 1858.

MY DEAR SIR:—In answer to your verbal inquiry, I would state that I was acquainted with John Fitch, *the steamboat man.* Some time after the revolutionary war, he came to my father's house, in Warminster township, to board, where he remained two or three years or more. Near the house was an old log shop, where my father carried on weaving, and James Scout, called "Scobe Scout," carried on silversmithing.

In this shop John Fitch built his first steamboat, which I distinctly remember, as I was a good sized boy. It was about four feet long, and a little over a foot in width, with a wheel in the stern, which was something like a flutter-wheel. When the boat was done it was taken to a dam on the farm of Arthur Watts, in Southampton township, near the present village of Davisville, and now owned by Gen. John Davis.

John Fitch was accompanied by James Scout, Abraham Sutphin, Anthony Scout, John McDowell, William Vansant and Charles Garrison. I went along, out of boyish curiosity, and after we had reached the dam, Arthur Watts, and I think his son William Watts, then a young man, came out to witness the experiment. I think the soft coal of Virginia was used to generate steam, and it is my opinion that the fire was lighted while the boat was on the bank. Before the boat was put in the water, the persons along were sent to the other side of the dam to prevent its running aground, and to turn it when it should come across. I was sent up to the head of the dam, where the water was shallow and the mud deep, as the men did not like to go in where they would get muddy. I waded in some little distance, where the water was deep enough to allow the boat to float, and stood there. The boat was launched, and in a few minutes it put off under full headway, puffing and the smoke flying, and very soon reached the opposite side of the dam. This run being too short, it was next started lengthwise of the dam, and made several trips back and forth to and from the point where I stood. When it reached me I turned it round, and headed it towards the starting point again. I could always tell about where it would come out when I saw it coming towards me, and waded through the mud and water to that place to prevent its running aground. We were there at least two or three hours, until all were satisfied with the experiment, when we returned home, Fitch carrying the boat. The gentlemen who witnessed the trial were delighted, and I was astonished. The boat had a deck, and I am certain the fire was below it, as it could not be seen when the boat was in motion. I think it had a smoke stack. The late Nathaniel Boileau, Esq., then a young man, turned some part of the machinery for the boat, and I carried it back and forth several times, and I remember I thought the wheels were pretty things, and wanted them for a wagon. I do not remember the year in which this took place, but I was born in January,

1782, and at that time I could not have been less than four or five years old. The whole transaction is indelibly impressed on my memory. Soon after this trial, Fitch took his boat to Philadelphia, where he met some person, and I am under the impression it was Fulton, who told him that some part of the machinery was not right, and that he had better alter it,—when Fitch returned home with the boat to make the necessary alterations, after which he went a second time to Philadelphia with his boat.

The shop in which this boat was built was on the farm now owned by Mitchell Wood, in Warminster township, within about three hundred yards of the county line of Montgomery county. Mr. Boileau lived at that time with his father on the farm now owned by Lewis Willard, on the county line between Bucks and Montgomery, near the eight square school house, and a little more than a mile from Davisville.

Yours respectfully,

Abraham McDowell, Warminster Township.
To W. W. H. Davis, Davisville, Bucks Co., Pa.

The writer of the above letter is a gentleman far advanced in years, and in perfect possession of his faculties. His character, among those who know him, is unimpeachable. It is the more interesting, coming, as it does, directly from a living witness of these experiments, and also strongly substantiates the many statements that have been made and published of this unfortunate man of genius.

The next boat that ran up the river after the *Phoenix* was named the *Philadelphia*. She belonged to the Union line, and was commanded by Capt. Jenkins. She ran from Chestnut street to Bristol, and afterwards established a wharf about three miles above, called "Van Harts," and thence in stages to New Brunswick and to New York in the *William Gibbons*. For some reason or other, this boat always went by the name of *Old Sal*. It is supposed that she obtained this name from the circumstance of her having a very grotesque looking female figure head, which, it is said, contributed but little to ornament her prow.

Next a new line was introduced, called the "Citizens' Line." The boat on this end was the *Pennsylvania*.[*] She ran to Bordentown, and thence in coaches to Washington, New Jersey, and thence in the *Ætna*, Capt. Robinson. This was in opposition to the Union Line. The *Ætna* exploded her boiler in New York harbor, May 12th, 1824, having on board the Philadelphia passengers; a number of lives were lost, and many badly scalded. Her place was supplied by one named the *New York*.

The Union line then built the *New Philadelphia*, to compete with the *New York*, of the Citizens' line, and then the *Trenton* came out to run against the *Pennsylvania*, of the Citizens' line, and then the Citizens' line brought out a new boat named the *Philadelphia*, to beat the *Trenton*.

---

[*] The engine of this venerable old boat is now in a tow boat called the *Lehigh*, running from Bristol.

There was a wonderful competition and even strife among these lines, which continued for several years, until Capt. Whilldin and Cornelius Vandergrift started an opposition against all of them. This was called the "Dispatch Line." The competition had become so great at one time that the fare was reduced to a dollar. The boat on this end was the *Emerald*. The Dispatch line was soon disposed of, and the railroad fever beginning to prevail, seriously affected the value of steamboats and stages. The Union and Citizens' line, with some of the others, ultimately became merged in the Camden and Amboy Railroad Company.

Since that day, there have been a number of up river boats, and some of them of a very superior order.

The *John Stevens*, one of the finest boats that ever floated on the Delaware, was built at Hoboken in the year 1846. At that time she was the largest iron boat in the United States. Her builder was Mr. John F. Starr, of this city. On the night of the 16th of July, 1855, she was entirely consumed by fire, when lying in her dock at Whitehill, near Bordentown. Her commander was Capt. Peter H. Kester. The *Richard Stockton*, by far the most magnificent steamer on our waters, and the largest boat that ever ran up our river, was built at Wilmington, Delaware, in 1852, by Harlan and Hollingsworth, highly celebrated builders. Her length is 30 feet longer than that of the *John Stevens*. Her commander is the young and accomplished Capt. Douglas Thompson.

There is one person attached to this boat who occupies a highly responsible position, and whose merits it would be injustice to overlook.

Who that has traveled up and down the Delaware river on this floating palace, does not remember to have seen at his post the sturdy frame of Peter Bloomsburg, the veteran engineer of the *Stockton*? The first account we have of Peter, he was a deck hand on board of the *Old Sal*, about the time of the war of 1812. In 1824 he went in the capacity of a pilot in the *Franklin*, and in 1825 he served in the same capacity on board of the *Trenton*. He is at this time, and has always been, the engineer of the *Richard Stockton*, and if we may infer from his present strong and athletic appearance, the indications are that he may be able to endure as long as the mighty machinery of that noble boat which he manages to control with so much power and skill.

As I have departed somewhat from my subject, by running up the river in these opposition lines, I will now return again to Camden, from whence I started.

You have been told, and let it not be forgotten, that the little steamer *Camden* was the first ferry boat of that description that ever agitated the waters of the beautiful Delaware. She was soon succeeded by another named the *Twins*, built by James Springer, and ran from the foot of Cooper street. She was constructed like two boats coupled together, with a propelling wheel in the centre, precisely like the renowned little *John Smith*, which plies so faithfully in the summer season between Smith's Island and somewhere on the opposite side of the river. She was commanded by Capt. Kellum, and owned by William Poole and James Springer. This

Capt. Kellum appears, at that day, to have been a very popular man. It is related of him that on one occasion he was the means of saving the life of a mother and child, by plunging in the river and rescuing both. For this praiseworthy act the "Humane Society" conferred on him a handsome present, in addition to which he was promoted to a more responsible position.

The next boat in order came the *Rebecca*. She was a very singular, and no doubt at that time considered of a very superior construction. She was named after the estimable wife of William Cooper, of Cooper's Point, from which place she plied to Arch street. She soon, however, lost this cognomen, and invariably went by the name of the *Aunt Becky*. Capt. Laning and Capt. Roth were her commanders.

There was something somewhat remarkable in the construction of the *Aunt Becky* that deserves a passing notice. Strange as it may now appear, she had a *wooden boiler*; it was clamped together like a cask; the flues were of iron, but the steam and water were enclosed within this wooden vessel. No doubt quite a competition sprung up between these rival boats which of them should excel in speed. I know nothing concerning the merits of the *Camden*, or *Twins*, but Captain Roth has informed me that he has frequently run the *Aunt Becky* from Cooper's Point to Arch street, in five minutes. If this be so, it is somewhat doubtful whether we have at this time a ferry boat on the river that can exceed this, not excepting the *Dido*, or the *Merchant*. In point of speed, we have gained but little by the substitution of iron for wooden boilers. This boat had also another nick-name, and that was the *Wheelbarrow*, from the circumstance of her having a large wheel at her stern, by which she was propelled. The next boat was the *Franklin*, commanded by Richard Fetters, Esq., of this City. She was built by Benjamin Reeves, who at that time kept the ferry at the foot of Cooper street; but afterwards removed to the Federal street ferry, and took with him the steamer *Franklin.* He also built the steamboats *Benjamin Rush*, and the *Lehigh*, which, like the *Franklin* and *Twins*, were double boats, having their wheels in the centre. After the removal of the *Franklin* to the Federal street ferry, the *Ridgway* appeared—a double team boat, propelled by nine horses walking around a circle. She ran from the foot of Cooper street. There was also a team boat named the *Washington*; she ran from Market street, Camden, to Market street, Philadelphia. Other team boats followed in succession, namely: the *Phoenix*, *Constitution*, *Moses Lancaster*, *Independence*, &c., &c.

There appeared to be a decided preference given to these *team boats.* One reason, it is said, was, they were considered more economical. In some of them, the horses numbered as high as nine and ten in number. They were arranged in a circle, on a tread-wheel connected with the main-shaft. By stepping on the wheel the shaft would turn, and thereby propel the boat. There was one great inconvenience attached to these boats, that would not suit very well the "fast ones" of the present age. Every day, at noon, there was an intermission of one hour, from twelve to one o'clock, which was devoted to feeding the horses. Whether some of our "fault finders" would be satisfied, at this time, to wait this period, until the animals had eaten their grub, is somewhat a doubtful matter.

A good anecdote is related of one of our old ferry masters, who was known to be of a jocose disposition. He had been annoyed for several hours by a swaggering fellow, who boasted of his great skill in the management of horses; that he could drive a single team better than any Jerseyman that could be produced. A wager was made by the landlord, that he had a single team of nine horses that he could not make go off a walk; neither could he tell the shaft horse from the leader. The braggart was taken down to the boat, where the horses were all arranged in a circle. He was asked to point out the leader. He cleared out at once to the city, in the "plaguy team," as he called it, and was not seen afterwards.

The next steamboat was the *Lehigh*, commanded by the late Captain Joseph Taylor, of this City. She was the first boat of any description on the river that adopted the use of anthracite coal in the place of wood. Next came the *Vigilant*. She ran from Cooper street, and was burnt up at her dock, after having run but a few weeks. She was followed by the *Delaware*. This boat was remarkable at the time, and attracted a great deal of curiosity, owing to her having a vertical cylinder, and a walking beam. She exploded her boiler in the dock at the foot of Cooper street, on the 31st of

October, 1837, producing the instantaneous death of John Thorne, the engineer, and frightfully scalding a Mr. Day, of Philadelphia. After great suffering, he expired on the fourth day after the accident. This appears to have been the first and only boiler explosion that has ever occurred among our ferry boats.

There was another steamboat, owned by Richard M. Cooper, Esq., named the *Camden*, being the second one of that name. She also ran from Cooper street. There was also a small steamboat called the *Minette*, alias the *Dandy*, Captain Kennard. She was undecked, and ran from the upper side of Market street, Camden, to an old ferry slip, between Market and Arch streets, Philadelphia; she was designed to carry passengers only, to and from the "Vauxhall Garden," at the corner of Market and Fourth streets, Camden, kept by Joseph Laterno, a Frenchman. She also ran in the evenings; but was soon abandoned as an unprofitable enterprise.

About the year 1828, Toy & Reeves built the *Philadelphia* and *William Wray*. They ran from Federal street slip, and succeeded the *Rush*. The *Philadelphia*, or rather the *Old Philly*, as every one called her, ran a number of years in conjunction with her old associate, the *Billy Wray*. She was never, in her best days, very remarkable for her speed; yet, she was a reliable boat, and by no means unpopular with the people. After a time, the "go-aheaditivenes" of the age soon began to cast the *Old Philly* in the back ground. There was one thing, however, for which she was eminently qualified, and for which purpose she was not unfrequently employed, and that was the carrying of children on "Picnic," Sunday School, and all other holiday excursions. How many young hearts have been gladdened, and how many eyes brightened, when the morning came, and they first saw the flag of the *Old Philly* waving, as though welcoming them on board, to enjoy a day of recreation and pleasure. The *Old Philly*, at one time, was in the honorable employ of "Uncle Sam," in surveying the site for the Delaware Breakwater. She has outridden many a storm at that bleak place, severely testing her strength and capability. Peace to her manes, she lies quiet at last, shored in a little by nook near Gloucester city. Since her day, there have been a number of other boats, namely:—*the Southwark, Citizen, Kensington, State Rights, Hornet, John Fitch, Cooper's Point, Kaighn's Point, Washington, New Jersey, Champion, William Penn, Farmer, Dido, Stephen Girard, Mariner, Merchant, Mechanic, Leo, Mary,* &c., &c.

The foregoing is believed to be a tolerably correct list of the various ferry boats that have plied on our river, commencing with the little *Camden*, and varying but little in the order in which they appeared. As has been heretofore stated, many of these boats, in past years, were laid up in their docks at the first approach of winter, and there remained until the opening of spring, during which period double ferriage was imposed on every traveler. Passengers at that day, as some may remember, were often subjected to great exposure, as well as detention, in crossing the river in the winter season. Twenty-five cents was always exacted from every one before the boat had left the slip, and beside this exorbitant charge, passengers not unfrequently, in icy weather, were compelled to work their passage over.

The *wherries* all had a long rope attached to their bows, at which every one was expected to lend a hand, if the ice was firm enough to sustain them; and often whether it was so or not. Some of you who were here about the winter of 1836 and '37, had an opportunity, as well as myself, of becoming tolerably well acquainted with these ropes. Ladies and children were kindly privileged to remain within the boat; but were not permitted, even in stormy weather, to raise their umbrellas, as they might impede their progress. As might be expected, they were not very precise as to the particular time of starting. The rule was, I believe, to hold on until they should get a load. With all these disadvantages, how could it be expected that Camden would improve?—the inducements were so few to dispose any one to adapt this as a permanent place of residence. What few Philadelphians came here to reside, were certain to return before the approach of winter.

————

INCORPORATION.

In February, 1828, Camden, by an Act of the Legislature, became a corporate town. At the passage of this Act her population was 1,143; in 1830, it had increased to 1,987; in 1833, 2,341; in 1840, 3,336; in 1850, 12,000. Its population at the present time is supposed to be over 15,000.

Her boundaries, as defined by the Charter, are as follows:—Beginning at the Pennsylvania line in the river Delaware, opposite the mouth of a small run of water below Kaighnton, running east to the mouth of said run; then up the same, crossing the public road leading to Woodbury from the Camden Academy; thence along the east side of said road to the road leading from Kaighnton to Cooper's creek bridge; thence along the side of said road to the middle of Cooper's creek; thence to the middle of the channel between Petty's Island and the Jersey fastland, or shore; thence down said channel and river to the nearest point between the States of Pennsylvania and New Jersey and thence to the place of beginning. These are the boundary lines of Camden. It has an average length of two and a half miles on the Delaware river; and one and a quarter in breadth, making an area of more than two square miles.

I have been more particular in giving the outlines of our City than would seem to be required, on account of the misapprehension of many on the subject. Our southern boundary is nearly the fourth of a mile below Kaighnton, to a small run of water; and northward to the Delaware river and Cooper's creek. Under the Act of Incorporation, the newly organized City Council held their first meeting on the 13th of March, 1829, at the Hotel of John M. Johnson, at the Vauxhall Garden. At this meeting there were present:—*Recorder*, John K. Cowperthwait; *Aldermen*, Gideon V. Stivers, James Sloan, Samuel Laning; *Common Councilmen*, Richard Fetters, Ebenezer Toole, John Lawrence.

Samuel Laning, Esq., was chosen the first Mayor of Camden; and was re-elected in 1829 and '30; previous to the expiration of the last year he tendered his resignation, which was accepted.

In 1831, 1832, 1833, 1834, 1835, 1836 and 1837, Gideon V. Stivers was elected and re-elected to the Mayoralty of Camden. The last named year the office became vacant by the removal of Mr. Stivers to Philadelphia in 1838.

In 1838 and 1839, Elias Kaighn was elected and re-elected.

In 1840, 1841, 1842 and 1843, L. F. Fisler was elected.

In 1844, by an Act of the Legislature, the City Charter was so amended as to give the election of this officer to the people. Under this amendment, John K. Cowperthwait was elected directly by the popular vote of the people.

In 1845, Richard W. Howell was elected; he declined, however, and the City Council appointed Charles Kaighn to fill the vacancy.

In 1846 and 1847, Thomas B. Wood was elected and re-elected.

In 1848, Benjamin A. Hamell.

In 1849 and 1850, Charles Sexton.

In 1851, L. F. Fisler.

In 1852, Charles D. Hineline.

In 1853 and 1854, L. F. Fisler.

In 1855, Samuel Scull.

In 1856, James W. Shroff.

In 1857, Benjamin A. Hamell.

In 1858, Clayton Trueax.

These are the names of all those who have occupied the Mayoralty of the City of Camden since its incorporation up to the present day; also the length of time they severally held the office. They are all still living with the only exception of Mr. Laning, the first incumbent. The City Council, with a highly commendable spirit, employed at once all their endeavors to enlarge and improve their new City, and to impart to it a respectable appearance. One of their early acts was to change the names of some of the streets, viz: King street was changed to Front street; Queen street to Second; Whitehall to Third; Cherry to Fourth; Cedar to Fifth; Pine to Sixth. Other improvements were effected, which naturally led to the introduction of others.

Council, viewing the necessity of having a suitable place in which to transact the business of the City, ordered the erection of the Town Hall on Federal street, in which the City Sessions were held, and beneath it is a "*lock-up*," which for years has been a "*terror to evil doers.*" An Ordinance was passed by the City Council of Camden, June 18th, 1828, for erecting this building; the following is a copy of it:

"SECT. 1. *Be it ordained by the Mayor, Recorder, Aldermen and Common Councilmen of the City of Camden,* That Samuel Laning, John K. Cowperthwait and Richard Fetters, be and they are hereby appointed Commissioners for buying a lot, and building a jail and court house in the said City, agreeably to their best skill and understanding, and which maybe the most judicious plan for our City; which said Commissioners, or any two of them, are hereby authorized and required to contract with such person or persons as may in their judgments be fittest to be employed in the building of the same, and to contract for such materials as may be necessary for the construction of the said building.

"Sect. 2. *And be it further ordained*, That the said Samuel Laning, John K. Cowperthwait and Richard Fetters, are authorized to borrow of Jacob Evaul twenty-five hundred dollars, at six per cent interest, for the above named purposes: *Therefore be it ordained by the authority aforesaid*, That the funds of the Corporation are hereby pledged and made liable for the payment of the money so borrowed."

The "City Fathers" should by all means preserve that old building; it is associated with the early history of our City, and has been appropriated to almost every conceivable purpose. There is scarcely a religious society, or one of any other description in Camden, that was not first fledged under that old roof.

Contrary to the expectations of many, the chartered privileges with which Camden had now become invested, added but little to her prosperity or advancement. She was too dead to be vitalized into life by a mere legislative enactment, or by the appointment of a Mayor, four Aldermen and five Common Councilmen. Before much progress could be anticipated, there was one requisite all essential to her interest, and that was more enlarged and superior facilities for crossing and re-crossing the river. At that day, as you have been told, the ferry boats were not of the character calculated to meet the wants of the community. During a part of the year, the only communication between us and Philadelphia was maintained by small row boats, which were entirely inadequate to meet the demands of the public.

The year 1835 opened a new era in the ferrying facilities of Camden. It was clearly foreseen that the difficulty of crossing the river, especially in the winter season, would more than likely prove a serious drawback on the opening operations of the "Camden and Amboy Railroad Company." The Messrs. Stevens were determined that these obstacles should not exist. Hence, a boat of great power was constructed at Hoboken, expressly designed to contend with the formidable masses of ice in the river Delaware. Many looked upon this as a most visionary and preposterous scheme, to suppose that the ingenuity of man was competent to overcome these stubborn obstacles of nature. Some declared it as impossible as it would be to attempt to propel a boat up "*Market street hill.*" But difficulties that had hitherto appeared almost insuperable, now readily yielded to the power of steam. Nobly did this *noble* boat, with her eighty horse power, more than meet the expectations of her skillful and ingenious projectors. This boat was the *State Rights*, or, as she was more generally called, the *Ice Breaker*. She came here from Hoboken, December 29th, 1835. To the "Camden and Amboy Railroad Company" (that "Monster Monopoly," as some have been pleased to term it), is not only Camden, but the whole traveling community, indebted for this first and great improvement in our winter transportation. Instead of being, at times, hours on the river, in an open boat, exposed to the severity of a winter's day, her passengers were conveyed across in from ten to twenty minutes, at half the usual price, with the comforts of a good fire and protection from the weather. This at once gave a final death blow to horse boats and wherries, and for years afterwards there might be seen their worthless old hulks, like skeletons, strewn along the shore; their decaying frames proclaiming to every passer by the incoming of the mighty *age of steam.* A few of the wherries were preserved and employed as night boats; not at five, ten or twenty cents a passenger, dollars were frequently demanded, or any sum that could be agreed upon with the ferryman, as he monopolized the night-crossing altogether. This at once gave a new impulse, and infused a fresh spirit of enterprise in our City, which has materially contributed to her growth and prosperity. Old sterile fields, which had hitherto been looked upon as valueless and useless, now began to rise in importance.

Nothing more retarded the progress of Camden than those insufficient means which had so long existed for crossing the river. How could she advance when bound down by such adverse circumstances? What Camden required, at that time, was increased and enlarged ferrying facilities; they were indispensable to her interests. The nearer the two adjacent cities were brought together, the more the interest and prosperity of both would be advanced.

The incorporation of a chartered Company called the "Camden and Philadelphia Ferry Company" is another element which has added greatly to the advancement of our City. The charter was granted in 1838, and the canal through Windmill Island was completed in 1839 and '40. This opened and established a direct communication between us and Philadelphia, which has proven highly advantageous to both. This at once led to the reduction of the ferriage; particularly to the quarterly passengers, which I believe (all things considered) to be the cheapest ferriage in America. One of the many impediments to the progress of Camden, was the impossibility of obtaining ground on which to erect dwellings. For many years, scarcely a lot of ground could be purchased in all North Camden, at any price. This induced one of our enterprising citizens to purchase a large amount of territory in the southern part of our town; this has been disposed of in building lots, on easy terms to the buyers; hundreds of persons have thereby been enabled, with a small amount of capital, to possess comfortable homes for themselves and families. This it was that so rapidly built up that portion of our City, which by many still bears his name. The march of improvement is still steadily advancing and expanding in every direction. Our river front, within a few years, has undergone a surprising change. Wharves have been extended far out into the river, and who knows but that this spirit of enterprise may go on until it shall stride over the Jersey channel, linking us still more closely together with our large and overgrown sister city, on the opposite shore. What would Camden be without Philadelphia—without an uninterrupted intercourse between us? A dead, lifeless and isolated town. Let the communication be entirely severed, and there is not an acre of ground in our City that would command ten dollars.

There have been no improvements in Camden which redound more to the credit and enterprise of our City Council, than that of causing the opening of Front and Second streets in the North ward. These streets are 60 feet in width, and are most beautiful thoroughfares, running in a direct line from Cooper street to the Delaware river, affording a most delightful view of the upper portion of Philadelphia and the surrounding country. Great improvements have already been made on these streets, many elegant buildings have been reared, ornamented with tasteful *parterres* in the front. This is destined, at no distant day, to become the most attractive portion of our City.

We are now steadily progressing. Within a few years a large number of dwellings have been erected, and many of them of a much larger and better description than heretofore. Not only houses, whole streets of houses have sprung up like magic around us. Where my own residence stands, and all about me, I have granted, in former days, (when in office,) poor old women the privilege to erect their booths and tents on the 4th of July, for the sale of their commodities. I have seen squirrels shot down from the branches of the lofty oaks, which then stood where now the Camden County Court House stands.

EDUCATION.

There are at this time a number of Seminaries of learning in this City, independent of the public schools in which all the branches of a thorough and substantial education are taught. These institutions are of a high order of merit, and are entitled to the patronage of the community.

Among the number, we would refer to that of Mr. J. D. Higgins. This is a male school, situated in a beautiful location, and which commands the respect of our citizens. The Rev. Mr. Powell, the successor of H. T. Wells, Esq., has recently opened that old established school under highly prosperous circumstances.

Among the Female Seminaries, we would call attention to those of Miss Janvier, Miss Powell, Miss Hodson, Mrs. Harris and Miss Glover.

THE PRESS.

The first newspaper published in West New Jersey, south of Burlington, was in Bridgeton, in the year 1794. It was called the *Argus*, and was published by James D. Westcott, Esq., the father of the present Postmaster of Philadelphia. After about two years this paper was discontinued, and another one was established in this place by John Westcott, a brother of the former, who continued it during the years 1803, 1804 and 1805. Its name is unknown. The next paper issued in West Jersey was the *Washington Whig*. It was commenced July 24th, 1815, by Peter Hay, Esq., now one of the aldermen of the City of Philadelphia, and senior editor of the press in that city. *The Washington Whig* was established through the agency of the "Washington Whig Society of Cumberland County," as the organ the Democratic party. Mr. Hay disposed of the paper in January, 1817, to William Shultz, a young man from one of the counties in Pennsylvania, who soon sold it to one John Clarke, in 1821, a pure native of the Emerald Isle. Clarke, in May, 1826, sold it to J. J. McChesney. In June, 1826, Robert Johnson, now of Philadelphia, purchased the *Whig*, and published it as the *Whig* and *Observer*. After about two years it was discontinued, but was afterwards revived by McChesney, who disposed of it to Franklin Ferguson, late of this city. Ferguson, in 1832, sold it to James P. Powers and James Newell. In 1834 S. S. Sibley, of Bridgeton, became the possessor. In March, 1837, Sibley transferred it to James S. Thomas, and Thomas sold it to Newell, and thus perished, after many long years of struggle and trial, this bantling of ten fathers.

The third paper which was published (in the now first district) was at Woodbury, in 1818, by John A. Crane, a brother to the eccentric Isaac Watts Crane, Esq., of Bridgeton. It was called the *Gloucester Farmer*. He continued it about two years, and then removed the press and paper to Camden. This was the first news-paper ever published in the City of Camden.

The fourth paper was the *Salem Messenger*, which was commenced in Salem in 1818, by Elijah Brooks.

In the fall of 1819, P. J. Grey, Esq., of our City, commenced at Woodbury the publication of a paper called the *Village Herald*. After a time he removed to Camden, and purchased of John A. Crane his interest in the *Gloucester Farmer*.

A few years after this, Samuel Ellis, an old school teacher, established a paper in this city called the *American Star*. This new luminary not shining very brightly, he concluded to dispose of it to Porter and Wollahon, who, fearing it might still become more dim, they wisely changed it to that of the *Camden Mail*. Their successors were Dr. Sickler and a person named Ham, from whom, in 1834, it passed into the hands of P. J. Grey, Esq., who has continued it and still continues it at the present time, under the name of the *West Jerseyman*.

Near 1830, Josiah Harrison, Esq., of this city, issued a little hebdomadal sheet called the *Republican*, which was continued by him for several years, after which time Franklin Ferguson became its proprietor.

In 1840 a new paper made its appearance called the "*American Eagle.*" It was published by Charles D. Hineline, who had his office in a frame building on Bridge Avenue next to Elwell's Hotel. This building was afterwards removed, and is now occupied as a dwelling house, in Weatherby's court, and the name is still visible upon it. Mr. Hineline connected with him in its publication Henry Curts, and afterwards sold out his interest to a man by the name of Bossee, and started West. Bossee sold out his interest to Curts, its present facetious editor, who then changed the title of the paper to that of the *Phoenix*, and still continues its publication with great regularity, *semi-occasionally*.

In 1846 Mr. Hineline returned from the West, and bought out Mr. Ferguson, who had, on the ruins of the *Republican* (Mr. Harrison's old Whig paper), commenced a paper called the *Dollar Weekly*. This sheet Mr. Hineline discontinued, or rather built upon it the present "*Camden Democrat*," the organ of the Democratic party in the First District, and continued its publication until July, 1853, at which time he sold it to Col. Isaac Mickle. Col. Mickle continued its publication until July, 1855, when, his health declining, he placed it in the hands of two practical printers, Messers. E. L. Garren and Wm. C. Figner, who continued its publication for him up to the time of his death, which took place in December, 1855. The paper was then sold, and Capt. Isaac W. Mickle, a cousin to Col. Isaac Mickle, became its proprietor, and connected with him C. D. Hineline, who was publishing a paper called the "*Spirit of '76*." This paper was merged into the *Democrat*, which accounts for the addition to its original title. Captain Mickle afterwards had associated with him James M. Cassady, and still later Mr. John Hood, its present gentlemanly editor, who has since become its sole proprietor.

Another paper of a more recent date has appeared, headed the *Camden Journal*. This is the organ of the "straight-out" American party, and is conducted by D. W. Belisle, Esq.

The first and only attempt to establish a daily paper in our City was made by P. J. Grey, Esq. Its first issue was dated January 4, 1858. It was named the *Camden Daily*, which was soon changed to that of the *Camden Evening Daily*. It was issued regularly from its commencement until Saturday, March 6th, in the same year. After a short lived existence of two months and a few days, it went out of existence for the want of a sufficient patronage, much to the regret of a large number of our Citizens. It is to be hoped that a similar effort will be made at no distant day, and one that will prove highly remunerative to its enterprising editor.

————

Camden, formerly in the district of Bridgeton, became a port of entry the 30th of June, 1834, during the administration of Gen. Andrew Jackson, who appointed Morris Croxal, Esq., the Port Surveyor. After which P. J. Grey, Esq., was appointed by President William H. Harrison. He was succeeded by Charles S. Garrett, Esq., under President Tyler. P. J. Grey was appointed by President Zachary Taylor, and Gen. Isaac W. Mickle by Franklin Pierce, and the present incumbent, Thomas B. Atkinson, by President James Buchanan.

————

Our ferrying accommodations have now become ample, and well calculated to meet the wants of the community. The *Dido*, and her ally, the *Mary*, are first class boats and for safety, convenience and speed, have no superiors on the river. The West Jersey Ferry Company, with their two substantial and beautiful steamers, the *Merchant* and *Mechanic*, have done much toward the advancement of Camden. All of the above boats are in a very superior order, and are not excelled by any other ferry boats on this river or on any other. That model hotel, the "West Jersey," at the foot of Market street, is unequalled by any similar establishment in this part of our State.

And even Kaighn's Point, that long neglected locality, one of the most beautiful on the river Delaware, is now in a flourishing condition. There are one or more excellent boats at this place, which ply regularly to South street ferry, and which command their full share of patronage.

For many years that part of our city had felt the necessity of a better accommodation for crossing the river. This resulted in chartering a new company, who seem determined to meet the wants of the community. A new ferry has recently been established at this point, carrying its passengers over to Reed street landing, near the Navy Yard. Its proprietor is Mr. J. Tuthill.

The time is not far distant when the eastern part of our city will present a very different aspect from what it now does. Cooper's creek, from its mouth upwards, will soon be studded with manufactories of every description, giving employment in all the various branches of industry.

Among the valuable recent improvements in Camden, is the introduction of gas in our streets and dwellings. It was first lighted on Christmas night in the winter of 1852. The Camden Water Works Company was chartered by our Legislature on the 11th of April, 1845. The water was first introduced November 1, 1846. Its capital is $50,000.

The streets which were first paved, were Federal street, and then Market street, both of which were completed in 1852.

Our facilities for traveling have been greatly improved by the attention which has been given to the streets and roads of our City. A number of turnpikes have recently been constructed, leading directly into Camden, which have materially increased the amount of travel throughout the county. There is one street, and that an important one, which, for some cause, has been entirely overlooked by our City Councils, and that is Broadway, the main thoroughfare into our City. It is doubted, whether, within a circuit of ten miles around us, there could be found a road of a similar extent in a more deplorable condition. If no other plan suggests itself, let it be turnpiked, and toll established on it.

There are at present three railroads which have their termini in this city, viz: The "Camden and Amboy railroad"; the "West Jersey railroad"; and the "Camden and Atlantic railroad." On the latter road there is a regular passenger train to Haddonfield, which affords great accommodations to the citizens of that flourishing section of our country. I met some time since the worthy President of the "State Bank of Camden" waiting for the cars to convey him home. "If anyone had told me," said he, "a year or two ago, that I should live to ride to Haddonfield, and from Haddonfield to Camden in a railroad car, I would not have believed it." In reply I could have said, "Had I been told that I should have lived to see Camden curbed, and graded, and paved, and supplied with water, and her dwellings and streets lighted with gas, and a new County Court House, which for design and durability will compare with any other in the State, I would have believed none of it." What Camden is destined to arrive at, no one can foresee or foretell; but if the coming future may be estimated by the past, then is she only in her infancy.

————

HEALTH.

The amount of population which Camden now possesses, demands of her still further measures to promote their interests and welfare; these should be early attended to by those having authority. It is believed that a well selected Board of Health should be established in this City, to whom the medical practitioners of Camden should report in writing, monthly, during June, July and August, giving a statement of the diseases which are prevalent, the number of deaths occurring, and other matters that may be deemed important. This would be attended with a very trifling expense, and would prove of the utmost advantage, and no doubt the physicians would willingly comply with it.

In connection with this, there should also be established a small hospital, or apartments for strangers or others who may become sick or suddenly injured by accidents, and have not the means of providing for themselves. The claims of humanity should impress upon the minds of the authorities the importance of these suggestions.

It is not outside of my province, nor without the range of my subject, to say some little concerning the health of our City. My profession entitles me to this privilege, and it is a matter in which we are all deeply interested. My readers are not unaware that by some, our location has been condemned as being very unfavorable to health. This charge, we take the occasion to say, is without foundation. There are persons who look upon Camden somewhat as they do on New Orleans, and pretend to believe that there is at all times an epidemic of some description prevailing among us. I have often heard them so express themselves, and one of the reasons assigned for it is, because our location is not on higher ground. I have yet to learn, after many years of observation, that the health of a city or community is dependent on its elevated position. Where, let me inquire, will be found the most fearful ravages of epidemic dysenteries, rheumatic affections, scarlet fever, and all the varied forms of bronchial affections? In our high mountainous districts. It is true, that at certain seasons of the year, intermittent and remittent fevers occasionally prevail; and I would ask where do they not? Even the City of Philadelphia in the autumn is by no means exempt from these attacks, though not unfrequently we are unjustly charged of being the cause of them.

It is feared that some of our medical brethren on the other side occasionally indirectly favor this supposition. If a decided case of intermittent or bilious fever happen to occur among them, does not the physician very frequently inquire of his patient if he has been to "Jersey?" If it happen to be so, the cause is at once accounted for, and we get the credit of it.

There is one fact that cannot have escaped the notice of medical men; it is this: when the autumnal fevers are prevalent among us, they also prevail in Philadelphia whether their patients have ever been to Jersey or not. Look at some of those beautiful mansions on the Schuylkill and in West Philadelphia. Many of them have been disposed of at much less than their original cost, and others remain untenanted a portion of the year on account of sickness; and yet we are told how very unhealthy is Camden. Whenever diseases of an epidemic character prevail with us, the same class also is found in that city, although marked with a higher degree of mortality. This fact is clearly evidenced by their bills of mortality.

―――――

THE WATER DEPARTMENT.

There is, perhaps, no one element which is more essential to the preservation of health than that of good, wholesome water; it is quite as important as it is that the atmospheric air we breathe should be pure and free from all imperfections. These are the two agencies, which, more than any others, it is believed exercise a powerful influence in promoting disease. Much has been said, and much written, in relation to the water with which our city is supplied. By some, it has been denounced as being very detrimental to health; while others seem disposed to ascribe every attack of disease among us, of whatever character it may be, to this element. This we deem to be erroneous. Any one who will take the pains to investigate this subject a moment, will at once be satisfied that there are other causes, as yet unknown, which are equally active in generating disease. For example, take the present season, when dysentery is prevailing among and around us in an epidemic form. Camden, comparatively, has suffered but little, when compared with some parts of the adjacent country; proving, without the shadow of a doubt, that our river water cannot be the only cause of its prevalence. Let it not be understood that I am advocating the purity of our water. Still I consider it much more harmless than that which is taken from many of our old and uncleansed pumps, which have stood until the materials of which they are composed are rotten and decayed.

The Delaware river water, if proper care be observed in administering it to our citizens, is at most times in a suitable condition for use, if we except on particular occasions, when it has been rendered extremely offensive, by heavy freshets, &c., which bring down a large deposit of vegetable and animal matter. This, of course, is unavoidable, and cannot be entirely remedied by the utmost precaution on the part of those who have the control in supplying it. This difficulty will occasionally occur, not only with us, but also with all other communities which are supplied by the Delaware river, or any other similar stream. While we are attributing to our hydrant water as being the cause of so much sickness, let us look and see if there be not other influences exerted, equally pernicious, and which are almost entirely overlooked, not only by our authorities, but by a large number of our citizens. Many of our cellars have not been ventilated nor thoroughly cleansed for years; the air having become so foul in them as to be almost sufficient to extinguish a lighted candle. How can a family expect to enjoy health when this state of things exist? Offensive sinks and cesspools, and filthy stagnant gutters are certain, especially in the summer months, to have their effects upon the health of our citizens. A poisonous effluvia is constantly arising from these places, which could easily be abated at a very trifling cost. By the exercise of proper sanitary measures, and a strict regard to cleanliness on the part of our authorities, Camden, much as she has been maligned and misrepresented by the designing, will, at no distant day, become one of the most desirable places of residence in our State. Her population is rapidly increasing, and improvements of every description are constantly in progress.

FIRE DEPARTMENT.

PERSEVERANCE FIRE COMPANY, NO. 1.

This was instituted March 15, 1810. It is the oldest Fire Company in our City, and on its roll-list is found a number of our most respectable citizens. After a lapse of some years it was revived in 1848. It has a number of active members on its list, and many others who sustain an honorary position. It has always been a very popular organization among the people, and has rendered very effective aid in some of our severest conflagrations. Its present President is Joseph D. Folwell; Treasurer, John Ross.

WECCACOE FIRE COMPANY, NO. 2.

The Weccacoe Fire Company, No. 2, was instituted October 7th, 1830, under the name of the "Fairmount." The engine was purchased from the Fairmount Fire Company, of Philadelphia, by a committee, consisting of Richard Fetters, Richard W. Howell and A. McCalla, Esqs. This company originated from the old Perseverance Fire Company, which was established as early as 1810. In 1831, the Company erected a house on the corner of Third and Plum streets. In 1835, the engine was rebuilt by Joel Bates, of Philadelphia, and her name changed to that of the "Niagara." She retained that name until 1848, when it was again changed to that of the Weccacoe Fire Company, No. 2, of Camden. The engine was purchased of the Commissioners of Southwark, at a cost of $750, in December, 1850, and in 1853 she was thoroughly rebuilt by John Agnew, of Philadelphia, at an expense of $850. On the 17th of February, 1854, their engine house, after several previous attempts by the incendiary, was burned down. This occurrence appeared to have no other effect than that of increasing their efforts to do good. In 1856, their new house was erected on Plum street, above Fifth. This is a substantial building, 18 by 60 feet deep, and is two stories in height. This Company numbers twenty-five active members and about thirty-six contributing members. She is reported to be in excellent condition. Her members are mostly young and energetic men, who at all times will be found ready to combat the terrible element which she is so well designed to encounter. Mr. James W. Ayres is her President.

SHIFFLER HOSE COMPANY, NO. 1.

The next Company in the order of time comes the Shiffler Hose Company, No. 1. This was instituted March 7, 1849. John R. Thompson, President, and George F. Ross, Secretary. Their house is a creditable building of brick, two stories in height, situated on Fourth street, below Walnut. They have two substantial carriages, one of which is almost new. Their charter of incorporation bears date September 11th, 1852. Samuel Brown, President. This Company, consisting as it does of a number of strong and spirited young men, is capable of performing a great deal of good.

NEW JERSEY FIRE COMPANY.

This Company originated from the disbanding of the "Mohawk." The first meeting was held at the house of William Garwood, in Cherry street above Third, May 1, 1851, and permanently organized by electing Henry Coombs President, and David H. Sparks Secretary. The following persons composed the organization: James Carr, Samuel Ames, David H. Sparks, Wm. Garwood, Thomas Butcher, E. B. Turner, Aaron Gibes, William Woodruff, John Wood, Henry Coombs, Adam Newman and Caleb Clark. At this meeting a committee was appointed to make application to City Council for the use of the engine formerly belonging to the "Mohawk," there being, at that time, no engine in South Ward for the protection of property in case of fire. This request Council complied with, and the Company immediately went into active service. At first the engine was placed in an old stable near Broadway and Spruce street, and run from there for some time, when it became apparent that the situation would not answer, and the Company removed to their present location, in Walnut street above Fourth. In September, 1853, a committee was appointed to procure a lot for the purpose of erecting a house. Nothing, however, appears to have been done in the matter, as we find that in September, 1855, two years afterwards, a similar committee was appointed, who reported in favor of and were ordered to procure a lot on Pine street below Fourth, for the sum of $250. This project also fell through, as the Company have since purchased the lot on Chestnut street above Fourth, and have ordered the erection of a two-story brick house, the second story of which is intended to be used as a hall for public meetings, societies, &c. The building, it is expected, will be completed about the first of October. The following is the list of Presidents, with the date of their election; Henry Coombs, May 1, 1851; James Carr, November, 1851; John Crowley, August, 1853; Joshua L. Melvin, May, 1854; Samuel Hickman, May, 1855; John Warrington, December, 1855; Jeremiah Brannon, May, 1856; Richard C. Mason, June, 1857; C. DeGrasse Hogan, May, 1858.

UNITED STATES FIRE COMPANY.

United States Fire Company is located in Pine street, between Second and Third. It was first organized July 4th, 1851, and bore the name of the Fairmount Fire Company, of Camden. Wm. C. Figner was elected President, Wm. J. Miller, Secretary, and John W. Hoey, Treasurer. It obtained its incorporation in 1852, and in 1853, by a resolution of the Company, its name was changed to that of the United States Fire Company, of Camden. James Scout was then elected President, and George Deal, Jr., Secretary. On July 1st, 1858, Wm. J. Miller was elected President, and George Watson,

Treasurer. This is a large Company, and one that has been very useful in our City.

INDEPENDENCE FIRE COMPANY, NO. 3.

The Independence Fire Company, No. 3, was instituted April 3d, 1851, and incorporated February 4th, 1854. Their house is located at the corner of Fourth and Pine streets. She has forty-eight active members and sixteen contributors. This is an active and efficient Fire Company, and has already proven very useful on many occasions in staying the destroying element. Her discipline is unexceptionable, and she is well calculated, from the number and activity of her members, to effect much good in our city. The "Independence," as well as all the others in the South Ward, are offshoots from the venerable old "Mohawk." Her President is Robert S. Bender, and Secretary, John Wallace.

WECCACOE HOSE COMPANY, NO. 2.

A new Company was organized on March 15th, of the present year. It bears the name of the Weccacoe Hose Company, No. 2, of Camden. This will form a very effective auxiliary, in case of fire, to the beautiful engine whose name it bears.

––––––––

We claim for our little State the respect and admiration of the whole Union. Her name is as unsullied as that of any other on the page of our country's history.

The part she bore in our struggle for independence should endear her to the heart of every true lover of liberty. I love Philadelphia much, I have many valued friends and relatives in that city, but I like New Jersey more. All the scenes of my early life, and of my riper years, are intimately associated with her. She is the land of my birth-place, and I wish her to be the land of my burial-place. General Washington paid her a compliment that was conferred on no other State in the Union. When he was retreating through the Jerseys, almost dispirited, her militia were at all times obedient to his orders, and for a time comprised the strength of his army. "My New Jersey regiments," said he on one occasion, "I can always rely on." These old veteran Jersey Blues, where now are they? They have nearly all gone

> "To join
> The innumerable caravan that moves
> To the pale realms of shade,
> Where each shall take his chamber, down
> In the dark and silent halls of death."

It has frequently been my lot to stand by the bed-side of some of these old revolutionary soldiers, and minister to them in the hour of pain and suffering. I have seen their dim and almost sightless eyes brighten up, and their furrowed cheeks glow afresh with pride and patriotism, when the stirring scenes of Trenton, Princeton and Monmouth have been called up in their memories. No one State of her territorial dimensions has produced a greater number of distinguished men than has our own. Among her sons we rank the bold intrepid Commodore Bainbridge, Capt. James Lawrence, Commodore Crane, Capt. Evans, Commodore Benj. Cooper, and Capt. James Cooper, one of the old veterans of Lee's legion. We also claim General Zebulon Pike, General Kearny, General Richard Howell, Richard Somers, the hero of Tripoli, and Commodore Robert F. Stockton, long distinguished for his daring valor.

Among her noted civilians are the names of Governor Williamson, Governor Dickinson, Governor Livingston, Governor Bloomfield, Chief Justice Kinsey, Kirkpatrick, Ewing, Elias Boudinot, Hornblower, Horace and Richard Stockton, Samuel L. Southard, James McPherson Berrian, Joseph McIlvaine, Frelinghuysen, Garrett D. Wall, Peter D. Vroom, Green, Warren Scott, Chetwood, Bishop McIlvaine, of Ohio, William L. Dayton, Stacy G. Potts, William Pennington, Miller, John R. Thompson, &c., &c. James Fennimore Cooper, the distinguished American writer, was born at Bordentown, and numerous others who have occupied prominent positions in our country. Not a few of them have gone to direct and adorn the councils of our sister States. A gentleman of this city, a few years since, visited the United States Senate Chamber, at Washington, and while there, there were pointed out to him six Senators, then occupying seats on the floor, all natives of New Jersey, viz: Dayton, Miller, Berrian, Breeze, Westcott and Henderson. Who was the great millionaire of Philadelphia, who did so much towards her improvement? Jacob Ridgway, an Egg Harbor boy, born at Leeds' Point. Who knows that the nucleus of Stephen Girard's immense estate was not formed when he was in business at Mount Holly. Who, at this time, stands at the head of Operative Surgery in our country? Dr. Joseph Pancoast, born near Moorestown, in Burlington County. Who is the distinguished Professor of the Practice of Medicine in the University of Pennsylvania; the successor of Rush, and Barton, and Chapman? Dr. Geo. B. Wood, a native of a small village in Cumberland County. Where was born the eminent criminal lawyer, who now adorns the Philadelphia bar, David Paul Brown? In Gloucester County, near Woodbury.

The time is fully within the recollection of many of us, when a number of the principal merchants of Philadelphia, were Jerseymen; they established for themselves a reputation for honesty, industry and integrity, which are still maintained by their descendants.

I have now presented my readers with an imperfect sketch of Camden, commencing with her early settlement up to her incorporation, and to the present day. My only object has been to secure some few of the local incidents connected with our city before it had become too late. It has been my endeavor to furnish facts alone, without the least disposition to deceive or mislead. For much I have had to rely on the statements of others, many of whom have now become enfeebled by age. If misstatements have been made, all I ask of my readers, is to ascribe them not to me, but to the infirmities and imperfections of human memory.

APPENDIX.

The Church of Macedonia was founded by Benjamin Wilson, and built in June, A. D. 1833. The number of members at that time was nineteen, and Ephraim Wilson was Secretary. Rev. Israel Scott was the first preacher. The present house, which is 26 feet by 60 feet, in Spruce Street below Third, was built in 1850; and the pastor, at this time, is Rev. Peter Gardner.

INDEX.

COLOPHON.

Numerous editing interns at Stockton University have helped to complete this text. Initial text preparation and editing was completed by Kristin Corum, Christina Gallagher, Sara Klemowitz, Jenna McCoy, Phillip Potter, and Ashley Rogers. Additional work was completed by Lauren Bork and Edward Arnold. Victoria Orlowski and Therese Reidy completed the final layout, design, and proofreading.

The body text is 12-point Bell MT. Cover design by the interns.

This is a publication of the South Jersey Culture & History Center. Our mission is to foster awareness within local communities of the rich cultural and historical heritage of southern New Jersey, to promote the study of this heritage, especially among area students, and to produce publishable materials that provide a lasting and deepened understanding of this heritage.

Additional Urban Histories
Published by SJCHC

Burlington Biographies: A History of Burlington, New Jersey, Told Through the Lives and Times of Its People
Robert L. Thompson

A monumental, 558-page history of Burlington from its founding by radical Quakers. Author Robert L. Thompson was formerly the Historic Preservation Planner for the City of Camden and brings his knowledge of architectural history and urban design to the task of understanding the city. Forty-seven chapters focus on the lives of prominent residents and city institutions. Lively storytelling and lavish footnotes will please laypersons and specialists alike. Only about 40 copies of this limited printing remain. 558 pages, hardcover with dust jacket. ISBN: 978-0-988873-9-3. $29.95

Atlantic City: Its Early & Modern History
Alexander Barrington Irvine ("Carnesworthe")

First published in 1868. Irvine, writing under the pseudonym "Carnesworthe," gave us the earliest history of Atlantic City. The work is filled with both humor and a steadfast belief in beneficent free enterprise. It provides readers with a romantic glimpse into the aspirations of Atlantic City's backers a mere fourteen years after the trains began running. 95 pages, paperback. ISBN: 978-0-9888731-0-0. $9.95. Also available in digital format $1.99 (Amazon)

Views of Pioneer Life
Daniel L. Risley

A reproduction of a rare 1896 sales prospectus for the Estelle Colony, a railroad-era real estate venture in southwestern Atlantic County (New Jersey), targeting immigrants and disaffected city dwellers with the promise of inexpensive, fertile, and profitable farmlands. The nation was emerging from the depths of the Panic of 1893. Much of the subdivision had been the property of the Estell family, purchased for this speculative venture by Daniel L. Risley. The introduction reads in part:

> "On the following pages are illustrations made from photographs of recent improvements in the place. You will find letters from some of the residents—the brave pioneers who have built their own homes and determined to be their own masters in a part of God's green earth where the sun shines brighter, the air blows sweeter and the ground gives forth more abundantly and more quickly on less outlay than anywhere else."

These claims were not entirely true. ISBN: 978-1-947889-97-2. $8.00

*9 7 8 1 9 4 7 8 8 9 2 3 1 *